Learn to Fold Origami

Insects

Katie Gillespie

www.av2books.com

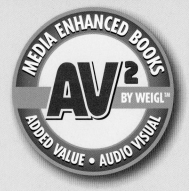

AV[2] provides enriched content that supplements and complements this book. Weigl's AV[2] books strive to create inspired learning and engage young minds in a total learning experience.

Your AV[2] Media Enhanced books come alive with...

Audio
Listen to sections of the book read aloud.

Key Words
Study vocabulary, and complete a matching word activity.

Video
Watch informative video clips.

Quizzes
Test your knowledge.

Go to **www.av2books.com**, and enter this book's unique code.

BOOK CODE

X77933

Embedded Weblinks
Gain additional information for research.

Slide Show
View images and captions, and prepare a presentation.

AV[2] by Weigl brings you media enhanced books that support active learning.

Try This!
Complete activities and hands-on experiments.

... and much, much more!

Published by AV[2] by Weigl
350 5th Avenue, 59th Floor
New York, NY 10118
Website: www.weigl.com   www.av2books.com

Library of Congress Control Number: 2013939644

ISBN 978-1-62127-678-4 (Hardcover)
ISBN 978-1-62127-679-1 (Softcover)
ISBN 978-1-62127-781-1 (single user eBook)
ISBN 978-1-48960-032-5 (multi-user eBook)

Printed in the United States of America in North Mankato, Minnesota
1 2 3 4 5 6 7 8 9 0 17 16 15 14 13

062013
WEP220513

Senior Editor: Heather Kissock
Art Director: Terry Paulhus

Every reasonable effort has been made to trace ownership and to obtain permission to reprint copyright material. The publishers would be pleased to have any errors or omissions brought to their attention so that they may be corrected in subsequent printings.

Weigl acknowledges Getty Images as its primary image supplier for this title.

Origami patterns adapted from concepts originating with Fumiaki Shingu.

Contents

6

2 . . . . AV² Book Code

4 . . . . Why Fold Origami?

5 . . . . Insects

6 . . . . What Is an Ant?

10 . . . . What Is a Bee?

14 . . . . What Is a Beetle?

18 . . . . What Is a Butterfly?

22 . . . . What Is a Cicada?

26 . . . . What Is a Ladybug?

30 . . . . Test Your Knowledge of Insects

31 . . . . Insect Adventure/ Key Words

32 . . . . Log on to www.av2books.com

10

14

18

22

26

Why Fold Origami?

Origami is the Japanese art of paper folding. The Japanese, and the Chinese before them, have been folding paper into different shapes and designs for hundreds of years. The term "origami" comes from the Japanese words "ori," which means "folding," and "kami," which means "paper."

Paper used to be very expensive, so origami was an activity that only the rich could afford. Over time, paper became less expensive, and more people were able to participate in origami. Today, it is an art form that anyone can enjoy.

It is fun to make objects out of paper. Before you start doing origami, there are three basic folds that you must learn. Knowing these three folds will help you create almost any simple origami model.

Hood Fold

Hood folds are often used to make an animal's head or neck. To make a hood fold, fold along the dotted line, and crease. Then, unfold the paper. Open the pocket you have created. Flip the paper inside out along the creases, and flatten.

Pocket Fold

Pocket folds are often used to make an animal's mouth or tail. To make a pocket fold, fold along the dotted line, and crease. Then, unfold the paper. Open the pocket you have created. Fold the point inside along the creases, and flatten.

Step Fold

Step folds are often used to make an animal's ears. To make a step fold, fold backward along the dotted line, and crease. Then, fold frontward along the dotted line, and crease. Repeat as necessary.

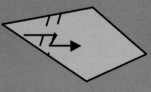

You will need:
- Origami paper (or any square-shaped paper)
- Colored markers or crayons

Practice making your favorite insects in this book to learn the skills needed to fold origami.

Insects

Insects have lived on Earth for four million years. They are the largest group of creatures in the world. Of the one million different animals that exist, about 80 percent are insects. Every year, scientists find up to 10,000 new types of insects. They believe that there could be as many as 10 million insect **species** still undiscovered.

Insects share many common traits. For instance, they all have six legs and two antennae. Their bodies are divided into three parts. These parts include the head, the **thorax**, and the **abdomen**. Insects do not have any bones. Instead, they have a hard **exoskeleton** on the outside of their bodies.

Insects have many special features. Some have colorful or patterned bodies. Others are more muted in color. Some have wings, and others do not. While some insects are thought of as pests, others are helpful creatures. They clean up after animals or make products such as silk or honey.

As you fold the origami models in this book, consider the different parts of each insect. Which parts are unique, and why? How would the insect survive without these features?

What Is an Ant?

Ants have lived on Earth for more than 100 million years. They can be found almost anywhere on the planet. There are more than 10,000 known species of ants. Most of these species live in tropical regions of the world. Ants are very strong. They can lift and carry several times their own weight.

Ants are social insects. They live in groups called "colonies." Each ant has a different role to play in the colony. The queen is the most important ant. She is the only one that can lay eggs. It is her job to lay enough eggs to ensure the survival of the colony. Worker ants are responsible for finding food. They also take care of the queen's offspring, help build the nest, and protect the colony.

Eyes
Ants have compound eyes. This means that their eyes are made up of many **lenses**. This makes ants especially good at seeing movement.

Stinger
Many kinds of ants have stingers or poison sacks at the end of their abdomen. They use these to defend themselves against **predators**.

Antennae

Ants use their **antennae** to help taste, touch, and smell. They also use their antennae to communicate. They do this by touching each other with their antennae. Ants use different signals to warn when danger is near or to tell which way to find food.

Legs and Feet

Ants do not have ears, so they use their feet to help them "hear." They do this by feeling vibrations in the ground. This helps them know when danger is near.

Stomachs

An ant has two stomachs. One stomach holds food for the ant. The other holds food for the ant's family. An ant stores food in its stomach until the ant reaches its family. Then, it spits out the food for the other ants to eat.

How to Fold an

Ant

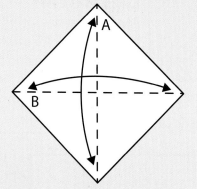

1 Fold in half along line A, and crease. Open the paper. Then, fold in half along line B, and crease. Open the paper.

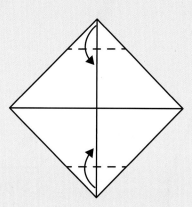

2 Fold the top point down one third. Then, fold the bottom point up one third.

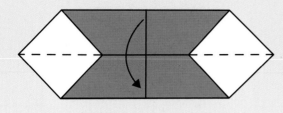

3 Fold the top down to meet the center line. Fold the bottom up to meet the center line. Then, fold in half, as shown.

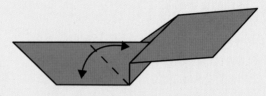

4 Fold backward along the dotted line, as shown, and crease. Fold forward along the same line, and crease. Unfold the paper.

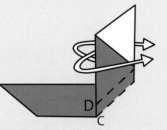

5 Hood fold on line C. Then, make another hood fold on line D, as shown.

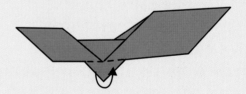

6 Fold backward along the dotted line, as shown, and crease. Fold forward along the same line, and crease. Unfold the paper.

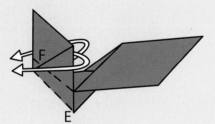

7 Hood fold on line E. Then, to make the ant's head, make another hood fold on line F, as shown.

8 Fold the bottom point inside to make a base. Repeat on the other side.

9 Make two pocket folds along the dotted lines, as shown. Finish the ant by drawing its eye.

What Is a Bee?

There are about 20,000 different species of bees. Some of the best known are honeybees and bumblebees. They make and live in homes called "hives." Honeybees are helpful insects because they **pollinate** plants and crops. Each honeybee can collect enough **nectar** to make 0.083 teaspoon (4.93 ml) of honey.

Most bee species live together in groups called "colonies." Just like ants, bees in the colony have different jobs. Worker bees protect the hive. They also find food. Worker bees are always female. They cannot lay eggs. Male bees are called drones. Their only job is to mate with the queen. It is the queen's job to lay eggs and to watch over the work of the other bees.

Wings
Bees use their wings to fly. Some bees make noise with their wings. A honeybee's wings flap 11,000 times every minute. This is why they sound like they are "buzzing."

Stinger
The best-known part of a bee is its stinger. Only female bees sting. This helps protect them against threats from other insects and animals. Bees use their stinger only if they are angry or upset. Some species of bees, such as honeybees and killer bees, die after stinging.

Body

Bees vary in size, depending on their species. Honeybees are about 0.5 inch (1.3 cm) long. Bumblebees can be twice that size. Most bees are shaped like ovals. Bees come in a variety of colors. Honeybees are golden yellow with brown stripes. Bumblebees are black with yellow stripes.

Eyes

Bees use their eyes to see. They can see every color except red. They can see some colors that humans cannot, such as shades of **ultraviolet**.

Mouth

Bees are **herbivores**. They eat **pollen**, flower nectar, and honey. Bees use their long tongues to suck nectar from flowers. They store it in their throats until they get back to the hive. There, they turn the nectar into honey.

Bee

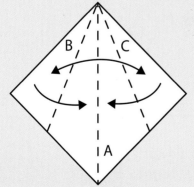

1 Fold in half along line A, and crease. Open the paper. Then, fold along lines B and C to meet the center line, as shown.

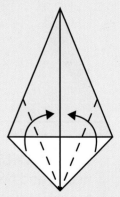

2 Fold the left side in to meet the center, as shown. Repeat on the right side. Then, open the pockets, and flatten.

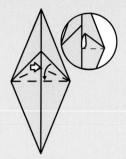

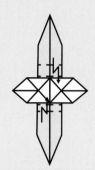

3 Open the right pocket at the white arrow, and flatten. Fold outward along the dotted line, as shown. Repeat on the left side.

4 Fold the right flap along the dotted line, as shown. Repeat on the left side.

5 Fold backward along line D, as shown. Repeat for line E.

6 Make a step fold on the top, as shown. Repeat on the bottom.

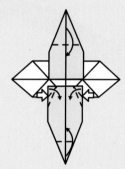

7 Open the left pocket at the white arrow, and flatten. Repeat on right side. Fold the top and bottom pointed along the dotted lines, as shown.

8 Open the left pocket at the white arrow, and flatten. Repeat on the right side.

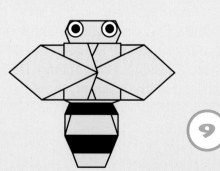

9 Finish the bee by turning it over and drawing its eyes and stripes.

What Is a Beetle?

Beetles are the largest group of animals on Earth. They are thought to make up at least 25 percent of the entire animal kingdom. In total, there are between 250,000 and 350,000 different species of beetles in the world.

Beetles can be found in a variety of habitats. They live in forests, deserts, grasslands, prairies, or on farmland. Some beetles make their homes under the bark of trees. Others live in saltwater or freshwater. Scarab beetles exist on every continent except Antarctica. They make up about 10 percent of all known beetles.

Wings

Adult beetles have two sets of wings. The back wings are the beetle's main flying wings. They are flexible and allow the beetle to catch wind better. The front wings are larger and more rigid. They are used to protect the flying wings and the beetle's body.

Size

Beetles vary in size depending on their species. Some small beetles may only be 0.08 inch (0.2 cm) long. Other beetles can be incredibly large. The Hercules beetle can grow up to 6.7 inches (17 cm) long. That is big enough to cover the palm of a human hand.

Color

A beetle's coloring can be important to its survival. Many beetles are shades of brown or black. However, some tropical beetles come in very bright colors and have detailed patterns. A beetle's color helps to protect it from predators. It lets the beetle blend in with the plants and vegetation in its environment.

Antennae

Beetles use their antennae in two ways. They use them to smell. They also use them as feelers, allowing beetles to sense what is around them.

How to Fold a
Beetle

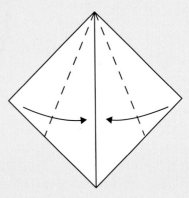

1 Fold in half along the dotted line, and crease. Open the paper.

2 Fold the left side in to meet the center line. Repeat on the right side.

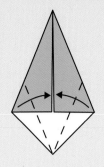

3 Fold the left point in to meet the center line, as shown. Repeat on the right side.

4 Open the left pocket at the white arrow, and flatten. Repeat on the right side.

5 Fold backward along the left dotted line, as shown. Repeat on the right side.

6 Fold the left side backward along the dotted line, as shown. Repeat on the right side.

7 Make a step fold forward, as shown.

8 Fold the top point backward, along the dotted line. Then, fold the bottom point backward.

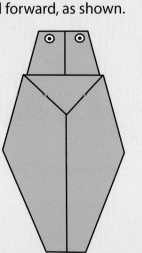

9 Finish the beetle by drawing its eyes.

What Is a Butterfly?

Butterflies can be found in most parts of the world. There are between 12,000 and 20,000 different species of butterflies on Earth. One well-known butterfly species is the monarch. It is easily recognizable by its black, white, yellow, and bold orange coloring.

Most butterflies are only active during the day. At night, butterflies sleep underneath leaves, inside rock **crevices**, or between blades of grass. Butterflies do not live for very long. The average lifespan of a butterfly is between one week and one month.

Color

The range of color among butterfly wings is huge. A butterfly's coloring helps protect it from predators. For instance, bright colors warn birds and other predators that the butterfly tastes bad. Some color patterns may also help hide a butterfly by allowing it to blend in with its environment.

Size

Butterflies range in size from 0.5 to 12 inches (1.3 to 30 cm). This is as small as a pin or as wide as a ruler. Butterflies weigh as little as two rose petals.

Antennae

A butterfly has two long antennae. Butterflies use their antennae for balance and to smell objects.

Mouth

A butterfly's mouth has a tongue-like tube that acts like a straw. Many butterflies uncoil their tongues to drink nectar from flowers.

Feet

Butterflies have six feet. Each foot has a special sensor on the bottom. Butterflies use these sensors to taste food. The front legs are often used to clean the butterfly's antennae.

Wings

Four fragile wings move a butterfly through the air. There are two wings in the front and two at the back. Most butterflies travel at speeds of 5 to 12 miles (8 to 19 km) per hour. The size of a butterfly's wings varies, depending on its species. They can range from less than 1 inch to 11 inches (2.5 to 27.9 cm) across. Monarch butterflies have a wingspan of 3.7 to 4.1 inches (9.4 to 10.5 cm).

How to Fold a
Butterfly

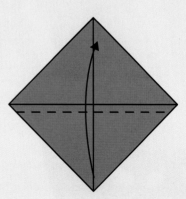

① Fold in half along line A, and crease. Open the paper. Then, fold in half along line B, and crease. Open the paper.

② Fold the bottom point up, along the dotted line, as shown.

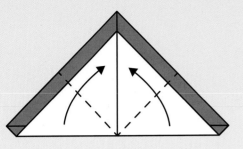

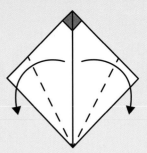

3 Fold the left side up to meet the center line. Repeat on the right side.

4 Fold the left side down, along the dotted line, as shown. Repeat on the right side.

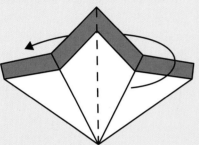

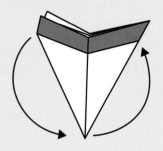

5 Fold backward along the dotted line.

6 Turn the butterfly over, as shown.

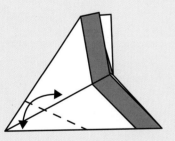

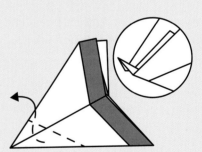

7 Fold backward along the dotted line, and crease. Fold forward along the same line, and crease. Unfold the paper.

8 To make the butterfly's head, make a pocket fold along the dotted line, as shown.

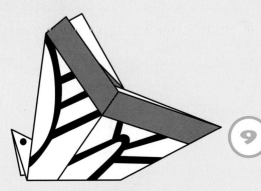

9 Finish the butterfly by turning it over and drawing its eye and wing pattern.

What Is a Cicada?

Cicadas are large insects with bulging eyes. They prefer to live in warm regions and can be found on every continent except Antarctica. Cicadas normally live in areas that are heavily wooded and have moist soil. There are between 1,500 and 3,000 different species of cicadas in the world.

Young cicadas are known to disappear into the ground. They will only reappear when they have finished growing and are adults. Some cicadas only take a year to develop. Other cicadas can stay underground for up to 17 years.

Wings
Cicadas have four clear wings that they use to fly. Their wingspan can be between 1 and 5.9 inches (2.5 and 15 cm). Male cicadas make a clicking sound by flicking their wings.

Head

A cicada's head is quite broad. It has two large compound eyes on each side of its head. Three more eyes sit on top of its head.

Beak

Some cicadas have long, thin mouths that look like a beaks. They use their beaks to suck fluids from plants. This is how they eat and drink.

Membranes

Cicadas are best known for the sounds they make. Male cicadas make buzzing and clicking noises that can be heard up to 1 mile (1.6 km) away. They do this by vibrating **membranes** on their abdomens. These sounds help them communicate with other cicadas. There are different calls for attracting a mate or expressing alarm.

How to Fold a
Cicada

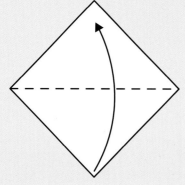

1. Fold in half, as shown.

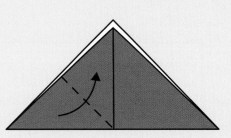

2. Fold the left side up to meet the center line.

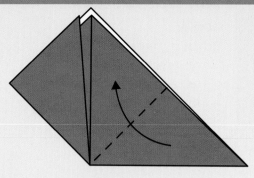

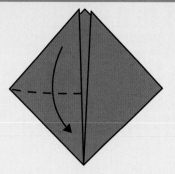

3 Fold the right side up to meet the center line.

4 Fold the left side down, along the dotted line, as shown.

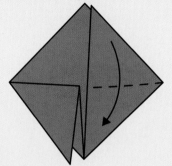

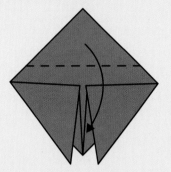

5 Fold the right side down along the dotted line, as shown.

6 Fold the front flap down along the dotted line, as shown.

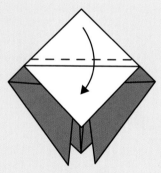

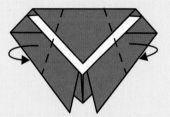

7 Fold the back flap down along the dotted line, as shown.

8 Fold the left side backward, along the dotted line. Repeat on the right side.

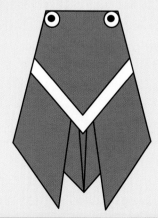

9 Finish the cicada by drawing its eyes.

What Is a Ladybug?

Mouth
Ladybugs have two strong jaws that they use to grab and chew food. Ladybugs can eat up to 75 aphids in a single day.

There are almost 5,000 different species of ladybugs. They can be found in Africa, Europe, Asia, and North, Central, and South America. Ladybugs can live in a variety of habitats, including forests, meadows, and gardens. In the winter, ladybugs **hibernate** in large groups. They have a life span of one to two years on average. In that time, a ladybug can lay up to 3,000 eggs.

Despite their name, not all ladybugs are female. It is difficult to tell male and female ladybugs apart. Females are usually slightly larger than males.

Legs
Ladybugs have six short legs. They secrete a yellow fluid from their legs, which makes ladybugs taste bad to predators. This is one of their best defenses against predators.

Size
Ladybugs range in size from 0.3 to 0.4 inch (8 to 10 mm). This is about the same size as a child's little fingernail.

Antennae

A ladybug has two short antennae. It uses them to help feel, smell, and taste. The antennae play a key role in helping the ladybug find its food.

Wing Covers

A ladybug's wings have their own covers called elytra. They vary in color depending on the species. Some are yellow, orange, or red, while others are completely black. Ladybugs are well known for having spots on their wing covers. However, not all ladybugs have spots. These bright colors and distinctive spots help protect ladybugs by making them unappealing to predators.

Wings

Ladybugs fly using their thin, transparent wings. They can beat their wings about 85 times every second. When not flying, the wings are folded into the elytra.

How to Fold a
Ladybug

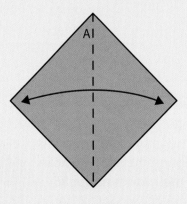

1 Fold in half along line A, and crease. Open the paper.

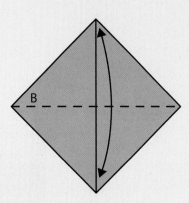

2 Fold in half along line B, and crease. Open the paper.

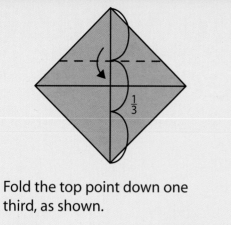

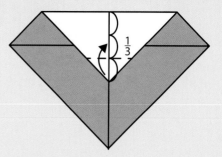

3 Fold the top point down one third, as shown.

4 Fold the point up one third, as shown.

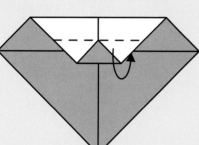

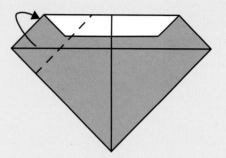

5 Fold inside along the dotted line, as shown.

6 Fold the left side backward along the dotted line.

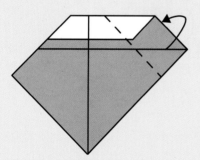

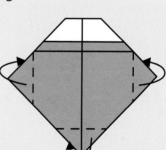

7 Fold the right side backward along the dotted line.

8 Fold the bottom point backward along the dotted line. Repeat on the left and right points.

9 Finish the ladybug by drawing its eyes and spots.

Test Your Knowledge of Insects

1. Which body part do ants use to communicate with each other?

Answer: Their antennae

2. What is a bee's home called?

Answer: A hive

3. How many different species of beetles are there on Earth?

Answer: Between 250,000 and 350,000

4. Why do some butterflies have brightly colored wings?

Answer: To warn predators that they taste bad

5. Why do cicadas disappear into the ground?

Answer: To grow into adults

6. How many eggs does the average ladybug lay in its lifetime?

Answer: 3,000

Want to learn more? Log on to www.av2books.com to access more content.

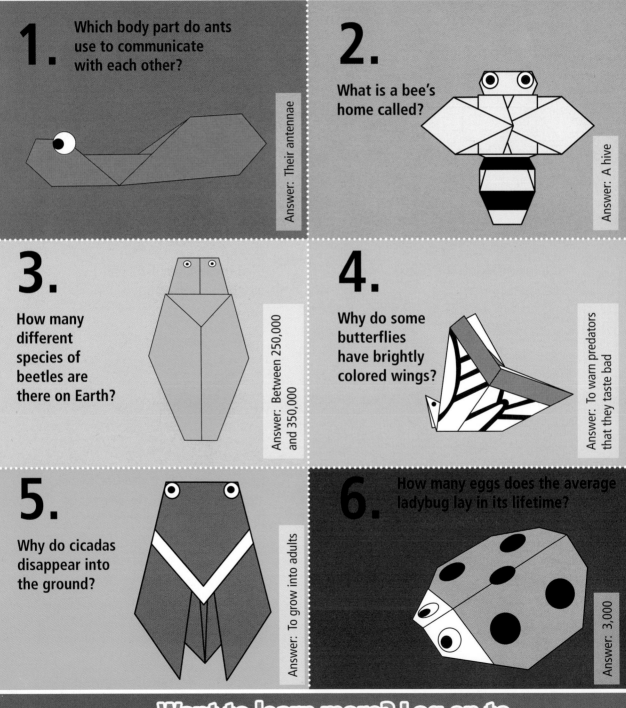

Insect Adventure

Materials
- Notebook
- Pen or pencil
- Magnifying glass
- Flashlight
- Gloves (optional)

Steps
1. Choose an area for your insect adventure to take place. Pick somewhere with trees or a pond. It can be a local park or even your own backyard.
2. Collect all of your adventure materials. Make sure you are dressed in boots, pants, and a long-sleeved shirt if you plan to explore wooded areas.
3. Look for ants, beetles, and other insects. Be sure to check under rocks, near flowers, or behind tree bark. Use your flashlight to help you check dark places such as hollow logs.
4. Use your magnifying glass to take a closer look at any insects or habitats you encounter. Be careful not to touch them in case they bite or sting.
5. Record your findings in your notebook. Write down the color, size, and shape of any insects you find. How many different insects can you discover?

Key Words

abdomen: part of the body where the digestive organs are found

antennae: long, thin body parts that extend from an insect's head

crevices: narrow openings

exoskeleton: a hard, outer structure that covers and protects an animal

herbivores: animals that eat only plants

hibernate: remain inactive for an extended time

lenses: parts of the eyes that focus images

membranes: layers of tissue that cover a surface

nectar: liquid food from plants

pollen: a fine powder produced by plants

pollinate: to transfer pollen from one flower to another

predators: animals that hunt other animals for food

species: groups of animals or plants that share certain features

thorax: the part of the body where legs and wings are attached

ultraviolet: rays of light that are invisible to the human eye

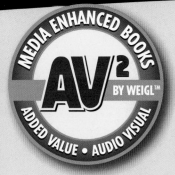

Log on to www.av2books.com

AV² by Weigl brings you media enhanced books that support active learning. Go to www.av2books.com, and enter the special code found on page 2 of this book. You will gain access to enriched and enhanced content that supplements and complements this book. Content includes video, audio, weblinks, quizzes, a slide show, and activities.

AV² Online Navigation

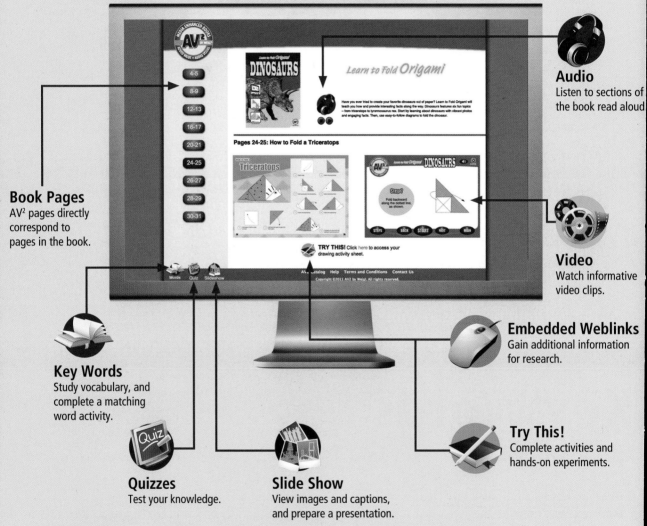

Book Pages
AV² pages directly correspond to pages in the book.

Audio
Listen to sections of the book read aloud

Video
Watch informative video clips.

Key Words
Study vocabulary, and complete a matching word activity.

Embedded Weblinks
Gain additional information for research.

Quizzes
Test your knowledge.

Slide Show
View images and captions, and prepare a presentation.

Try This!
Complete activities and hands-on experiments.

AV² was built to bridge the gap between print and digital. We encourage you to tell us what you like and what you want to see in the future.

Sign up to be an AV² Ambassador at www.av2books.com/ambassador.

Due to the dynamic nature of the Internet, some of the URLs and activities provided as part of AV² by Weigl may have changed or ceased to exist. AV² by Weigl accepts no responsibility for any such changes. All media enhanced books are regularly monitored to update addresses and sites in a timely manner. Contact AV² by Weigl at 1-866-649-3445 or av2books@weigl.com with any questions, comments, or feedback.